The Bank
of MOM is
Now Closed

LYNDA HYKIN

ISBN-13: 978-1499322132
ISBN-10: 1499322135

PEOPLE ARE TALKING ABOUT THIS BOOK!

"Brilliant!" says Dr. Bobby Chaudhuri, co-author of "Medical Maladies"

James Malinchak, featured on ABC's hit TV series Secret Millionaire says, *"If you want to take control of your life, buy Lynda's book!"*

LYNDA HYKIN

ACKNOWLEDGMENTS

My virtual mentors T. Harv Ekker, Jack Canfield, and the late Jim Rohn have all made a profound and positive impact on my life. That impact has resulted in this book and I am most grateful.

I would also like to acknowledge Bruce Outridge Productions, www.bruceoutridgeproductions.com for the amazing Teenage Money Magnet logo that has found its way onto the cover of this book.

I especially want to acknowledge all my grandchildren, who I continue to learn from everyday; about peace, joy, and living just for the moment, with no regrets, no prejudice and no fear.

With my family and friends in my life, I am already wealthy beyond my wildest imagination.

To Moms

- What if your Teen never asked you for money?

- What if they graduated from College or University debt free?

- What if money was not a 'hot button' that got pushed?

- What if you knew your Teen would never have to worry about their financial future?

To Teens

- What would you do if you suddenly had no Bank of Mom?

- What if you didn't **need** the Bank of Mom?

- What if you had your own bank?

- What if you had a solid financial future?

Inside this book are 10 Secrets that may be the answer to all the above.

LYNDA HYKIN

DEDICATION

To my Grandchildren. May you always:

Live with intent

Walk to the edge

Play with abandon

Practice hard

Listen well

Choose no regret

LYNDA HYKIN

LYNDA HYKIN

READ THIS FIRST
(PREFACE)

Who am I and why do I believe I have the qualifications to write about money?

For starters, I wrote the book on what NOT to do with your money. Seriously, I wrote a book on it! I wrote the book because I *lived* by what I wrote in the book! I lived my entire life pay cheque to pay cheque. I never saved money. I didn't think I needed to. Life was easy. I was going to be young forever. I could quit any job I didn't like and find another immediately. If I couldn't pay my rent, I moved. Money was never an issue... because I always managed to earn it.

This 'money' philosophy carried on long after my wild, single days were over, continued even when I was married and then when I was raising my daughter as a single mom. Like handing down the great gifts of my Ancestry, I taught my daughter how to live pay cheque to pay cheque, just like me. I showed her how to spend anything that was left over... if there *was* anything left over (never was), to never save and always be broke.

I was a master at spending FIRST and then paying whatever I could with whatever was left over. My financial plan went something like this:

- Pay day

- Spend all my money

- Broke for the next two weeks

- Payday - So excited to have money again I celebrated by spending all my money

- Broke again. Do you see a pattern here? (This is a clue.)

When little bits of unexpected money came in...Yippee! I spent every last cent! After all, it was extra and so it should be just for me! There were times when I didn't know how I was going to pay the rent, or feared that I would lose my house. There were times when I didn't have money to put food on the table. There were times when the gas was shut off and I had to shower at the Y.

In 2001, I received a severance package of something just shy of $100,000.00. Within 2 years, I was broke. In 2006, I received an inheritance of about $65,000.00. Within 2 years, I was broke. In fact, I sold everything I owned and got ready to move into my new place....

Yep! This was about to become my new living quarters, AND I suddenly found myself no longer young, with no job and unable to find work. Apparently while I was busy living pay cheque to pay cheque I got older. I was no longer prime hiring material.

I was on my own - broke, homeless and terrified.

Desperate times call for desperate measures. I was now 55 years old. Most 55 year olds were setting plans in motion to retire and enjoy their life. Not me. I was starting from scratch – again. I took the money from the sale of all my Worldly Possessions, including my vehicle (which added up to approximately $1500) and flew completely across the country... to a place I had never been before, with no money, no job, no home and no friends.

It was one of the best decisions of my life. I spent the next 3 years personally developing and learning. I listened and learned everything I could about being successful, about becoming a brilliant and savvy business woman, creating a new mental attitude, a new philosophy about who I was and who I wanted to be. I removed old, bad habits and developed new, healthier and better ones. I was meeting and having casual conversations with millionaires. I was like a sponge, soaking up information given freely from highly successful people (clue), watching what they did, who they hung out with, who were THEIR mentors, what qualities did I like about them that I wanted for myself. (clue)

Yet, even after all of this, with all my new-found knowledge, I *still* spent my money like I always had. [Insert the word duh! here.] Make it, spend it, broke. Make it, spend it, broke. I knew that I had to change this cycle, that I no longer wanted to live like this.

I finally clued in that it wasn't my bank account that needed to change or my job or my opportunities, or that one really big break that would fix everything. It was me. In order for things to change, **I** had to change. I had to find out **why** I did what I did so I could fix it, replace it with choices and new beliefs that allowed me to grow not just mentally, but financially. I did and it worked.

In this book are the secrets to what I did and how I made it work.

My plan is to share this information and hope that it does the same for you. Before you even finish high school, I want you to learn the Secrets that can make you rich and successful, financially literate and financially free. Discover in these pages, the habits of the wealthy.

If you do...

You will never have to go to the Bank of MOM again because you will have opened your own.

So what's this book about?

It's about money. It's about how to earn, save and grow your money. It's about breaking free of the poverty cycle, and creating your own financial freedom.

It's about you.

LYNDA HYKIN

CONTENTS

	Introduction	Pg # 19
Secret #1	**Do you speak 'Money'?**	Pg # 29
Secret #2	**What are you thinking?**	Pg # 47
Secret #3	**Do the Math**	Pg # 63
Secret #4	**What do you do with a Dollar**	Pg # 75
Secret #5	**Profits are better than wages**	Pg # 83
Secret #6	**Breaking the Poverty Cycle**	Pg # 99
Secret #7	**The Plan**	Pg # 117
Secret #8	**The Gratitude Attitude**	Pg # 133
Secret #9	**Be Rich or be Wealthy**	Pg # 147
Secret #10	**Your Future is Blank**	Pg# 155
	Support and Resources	Pg# 167

LYNDA HYKIN

READ THIS NEXT
(NO, DON'T SKIP TO THE 1ST CHAPTER!)

INTRODUCTION

Welcome to the Big Leagues.

High school is NOT Grade school. There is no more recess. There is no-one to comfort you when you fall and skin your knee. You may be supplied with a band-aid but **you** will have to clean the wound yourself, know enough to disinfect it, and apply the band-aid onto the appropriate spot.

High school will provide information on a variety of subjects, but **you** will have to decide what, if anything, to do with that information. Lessons will be taught to expand your mind and supply you with fundamental knowledge.

It will leave you clues to your future. But **you** have to learn how to recognize those clues and use them. (I will continually drop 'clues' throughout this book. Consider these little extra nuggets of gold that you should pay attention to.)

You will find out what subjects you like, what subjects make you fall asleep and what subjects make you wonder what language the Teacher is speaking, because you just don't get what they are talking about.

21

You may discover you have a talent for Drama, Photography, Art or Music. You might figure out that extracurricular activities such as basketball or soccer are something you rock at. You may learn that without a doubt, history is *the* most boring subject EVER and the information is totally useless to you. The Yearbook committee, Class President or Fund Raising events may awaken hidden interests, never known to you before. You may even find out... you want to TEACH!

Different subjects and activities will be offered to you, and you will be able to pick and choose; take what you like, drop what you don't like. You will find out what you are really good at, and what you really suck at, and these choices will help you make some decisions about your future.

There will be all kinds of different subjects for you to learn about.

Money will *not* be one of them.

The subject called Money; how to manage money, how to earn, keep and grow your money will not be on the list of crucial lessons you need to learn before you head out into the big, wide, scary world on your own. It's one of the most important life skills, yet it has never been taught in schools.

Whether your current ambition is to:

- Live with your parents for the rest of your life off their money and hope THEY move out
- Assume that once you graduate the money will just show up
- Work at McDonald's as a long term career choice
- Turn into a life-long student
- Become Prime Minister
- Become a Millionaire
- Own your own business
- Become an Inventor of the greatest thing ever invented
- Be the scientist/doctor that discovers a cure for ALL disease

... you will need money. Your high school, the college or university you plan on attending will not teach you how to acquire that money.

I will.

This is Money 101. Within lies the Secrets to your Financial Future.

I called the Chapters 'Secrets' because most of us don't know any of this information. It is not freely shared and if we have heard about it, we don't know how to use it.

This is your opportunity to break the poverty cycle, to learn how to make the most of every penny you will ever earn so you can achieve the financial freedom everyone wants, but few obtain - in the shortest, fastest, most direct way possible, just by learning and following the information in this book.

My wish is that after you understand and use the information, you no longer keep it a secret but that you go out and share it with everyone.

So, step one.

Do you REALLY want more money in your life, more success? You may think that's a stupid question, but as you read this book, you will find out that it's not a stupid question at all.

Are you WILLING to pay attention to the secrets in this book?

Will you make a commitment, to yourself, right here and right now that you will take these secrets and apply them to your life, no matter what?

If so, sign the commitment pledge on the next page. You can also go to the Teenage Money Magnet™ website, and print out the 'cool' version, frame it and hang it on your wall.

Don't want to sign it? Think you'll wait until you read the book first? No problem. That's okay.

(You are the one I wrote this book for!)

As a gift from me to you, go to theteenagemoneymagnet.com and you will find ALL the printouts and exercise sheets from the book in the TMM Members Only Section. The membership is free as a thank you for purchasing (and reading) the book!

They are also in the back of this book, under the various chapter headings.

Also, as an alternative to writing in this book, I suggest you go to the dollar store and pick up a notebook to write down your answers, thoughts and inspired ideas.

This is part of the commitment – to be fully engaged in the process laid out for you over the next 180 or so pages. A little time taken now for a lifetime of living the life you desire. I think it's worth it.

LYNDA HYKIN

COMMITMENT PLEDGE

I, being of sound mind and body, do hereby pledge to commit to no longer allow myself to be subject to living an ordinary life. I will not stifle my opportunities for growth and improvement, or inhibit my access to the miraculous and incredible potential lying inside me that will lead me in the direction of my greatest dreams, desires and ambitions and allow me to make a profound difference in my life, the life of my family and the world around me.

I do hereby commit to read and apply the information in this book. I will participate by reading the information, and completing all exercises.

_____

Signature

Date _____

LYNDA HYKIN

LYNDA HYKIN

SECRET #1

DO YOU SPEAK MONEY?

Money has a language of its own. I'm sure you've heard it spoken:

- We can't afford that

- Money doesn't grow on trees

- I'm not made of money

- We're broke

- I don't have enough

- We have to wait until pay day

- It costs too much

- Rich people are greedy

- The rich get richer while the poor get poorer

- It's the ...insert here ...
  governments'/bosses'/parent's/ their/ ... fault

- If I won the lottery then I would be happy

- You have to work hard for everything and anything

- Live within your means

There are many other words and phrases to the language of money but these are the some of the most common and have been spoken over and over for generations – generations of poor people, unsuccessful people, broke and unhappy people. They don't know or understand the language spoken by the successful, the wealthy, and the rich, because they have never heard it spoken around them; among their family and friends and co-workers.

We understand the language that is spoken within our own culture day in and day out on a regular basis. It's all that we've been taught. It's the same with 'money' language. You speak and understand what you have heard and what you've been taught. What happens when you are thrown into a culture where you don't understand the language? You're frustrated, angry, sad … maybe even frightened. You can't do anything, because you can't get people to understand you and you don't understand them.

The same holds true with the language of money. If you don't understand it then you aren't able to live in a culture of money. The rich get richer because they understand the language of the rich; they speak and believe in the language of money. And knowing that language is how you earn, keep and grow money.

You also have to be **willing** to learn the new language if you want to speak it.

Can you learn a different language? Absolutely.

Can you learn a different money language? Absolutely.

You can learn a new language through books, Videos, CD's – all kinds of different ways. These are some great ways to learn something new. But the shortest, quickest, most direct and best way is to immerse yourself in it, surround yourself with people that speak the same language as the one you want to learn. Do what they do, say what they say, spend time understanding the new language every day. Soon, you will speak the same language fluently without hesitation.

I am going to help you speak a new money language, the one that successful people speak.

NOTE: It will not make you 'bi-lingual'. This is different. There is no bi-lingual when it comes to money. You want to **remove** the old language and **replace** it with the new and only speak the new from now on.

It's okay to notice and be aware of the old language you used to speak, because that shows you how far you have come. It's funny when I hear people say certain phrases or talk about money the way I used to, I think, 'Wow, not too long ago that was the way I talked.' But now I have a new 'money language' and I'm going to share it with you.

In order to do that, you have to be *willing* to learn something new. You have to be willing to change. Are you? Jim Rohn, one of the great philosophers said, "In order for things to change, *you* have to change." Not the Government, not the teachers, the Corporations, your parents - but *you*.

Got it? Because this is crucial. Nothing else will make sense, or will work unless you understand that you have to talk 'money' differently, do things differently and see things differently… and THINK differently.

Lesson 1

What are you always saying about money?

Write it down. Oh, that reminds me. Get a notebook. You're going to be doing a lot of writing stuff down.

For one week, track whatever you catch yourself saying about money, good and bad. Also write down everything you HEAR being said about money, the good and the bad.

You can split a page if you want, and put all the good stuff on one side and all the bad stuff on the other, like this:

THE GOOD STUFF	THE BAD STUFF
I earned $10 today!	I can't go 'cause I don't have any money.
I'm going to save up for...	I'll never be able to have …..

At the end of the week count it up.

- How many times did you say something positive about money? _____

- How many times did you say something negative?_____

- How many times did you say THE SAME THING over and over? _____

This is your starting point. Pick 3 things that you notice you said or heard the most. We'll work on those first.

Now turn them around.

Again, split the page in half. Write the negative comment on the left, and on the right, write down the opposite, a positive comment, like this:

I never have any money.	I always have money.
My friends are always broke.	My friends have money too, like me.
Working sucks.	I love earning my own money.

Make these comments personal for you, write them down like you would say them. I can't do that for you because I don't know you personally. It can even be as simple as; I don't have money....I DO have money. I will never be rich. I am GOING TO be rich.

Even if you don't really believe the right hand side yet, do it anyway.

Then for the next 30 days (clue), be aware of what you are saying about money. If you catch yourself speaking the old money language replace it immediately with the new. If you hear something negative about money, change it in your head. Have fun with this! It is not supposed to make you feel bad when you use the old language, it's supposed to make you smile when you catch it and replace it with the new!

Do not beat yourself up if you slip – because you will. I still catch myself! When you think you've mastered one, replace it with another on your list. Don't forget about the first one, keeping doing that one plus another. Go through the entire list. No, it won't take forever! (yes, I can read your thoughts!)

The funny thing about this exercise, is once you start talking in a more positive way about money, more positive expressions about other things will automatically start to push out the negative ones.

I have no idea how this works, but it does. (Okay I do, but that's not the lesson here, we'll talk about that later.)

Kevin Trudeau had a quote that has stuck with me ever since I heard it about 5 years ago. It was, "You don't know what you don't know."

Meaning if you don't know that you are always speaking negatively about money, if you're not aware of it, then how can you possibly know to change it??

BTW, this works for EVERYTHING in your life, not just money. If you want something different (better) in your life, you have to understand that there is something you don't know about it. You have to 'know' that you 'don't know' something; what to do, how to change it, who to ask, whatever. Even something as simple as just speaking differently about it.

I can prove it.

If you knew all there was to know about money…wouldn't you have money? Do you think maybe there is something about money you don't know, and that if you did know it, you would have it?

Now you know that you don't know. And that's okay. Because the cool part is, someone out there does know about money. And they are more than willing to teach you. Clue. (That comes later in the book too.)

Here is something I want to tell you up front and right at the beginning of this book:

Money is just a tool. It is simply a 'thing' that we use to help us get what we want. Unfortunately, everyone attaches EMOTION to money. Money by itself is neither good or bad. It's just a thing, a piece of paper. Before money came along, people used goats and chickens to obtain things they wanted. Some places still do. You need to stop attaching **emotion** to money. Emotion is a feeling – money is a thing.

I know that this is very difficult to do, especially if you live in poverty, if there is no money to put food on the table or a roof over your head. But because society is so wrapped up in the money=happiness illusion, they stop looking at other ways to achieve what we all want - happiness, freedom. That freedom includes personal, emotional, spiritual, financial and even physical freedom from pain/hurt/anger/fear. We just think the only way to achieve all that is to have lots and lots of money.

Wrong.

"But…" you say, "If I have money I'm happy and if I don't have money, I'm sad." Not really. You can be happy without money. You can be sad with money.

It's what you THINK about money that makes you happy or sad. I'm really not trying to get too 'deep' or philosophical here, but think of money like a car. A car is one way of getting where you want to go. There are many other ways to get there as well.

Let's say I gave you a suitcase with a million dollars in it, and told you to stick it under your bed and leave it there – forever. You are never allowed to touch it or spend any of it. Are you rich? You have a million dollars. That makes you a millionaire, right? If you told people you had a million dollars 'tucked away', they would think you are very rich! But you're not, not really. You still have to go out and earn money to pay your bills and to live. **Having** money doesn't make you rich or happy. It's what you **do** with the money that can make you wealthy. It's what you **do** that can make you happy.

You have an opportunity to develop the right money language and the right mindset about money **before** too many bad habits, thoughts, and emotions get you all tangled up in the drama of money. Start now to think about money for what it really is – simply a vehicle that you use to get you where you want to go. Something you use to help others, make the world a better place.

Start thinking that it's **okay** to have money and that the more money you acquire, the more good you can do with it.

- How many people can you help with one dollar?

- How many people can you help with $100,000? A lot more I suspect.

- And if you had more money, could you offer more ways to help others help themselves? (clue).

Start learning the POSITIVE language of money. The more you speak it, the more you will understand it. The more you understand it, the more comfortable you will be around it and the more you will bring into your life.

Positive thoughts attract positive things. Negative thoughts attract negative things. I find it fascinating that grown-ups don't believe in the power of positive thinking, yet almost all believe in the power of negative thinking.

Here's a test. Ask your parents, or an adult if they know what Murphy's Law is. Most will be able to tell you. Murphy's Law states that whatever can go wrong

– will go wrong. If you day starts out bad, most people believe the rest of their day will go bad. Ever hear someone say, " I should have stayed in bed."? Well, if that's true, why can't the OPPOSITE be true? Whatever can go RIGHT, will go right? Start thinking positively about money. Start making positive statements about money. I do deserve to have money. I can have that ….(fill in the blank). Here's a good one to write down and repeat several times a day, especially when things aren't going well: "I **can** have, do or be **any**thing I want."

I know it wouldn't be cool to carry it around with you, but maybe write it in one of your notebooks, or post it on your bedroom wall.

Money language is learned. It's not inherited or given to only a 'select' group of special people. ANY one can learn it.

And now you know that you can learn it too.

LYNDA HYKIN

QUICK SUMMARY:

- What are you repeatedly saying and hearing about money?

- What are your friends and people you hang out with saying about money?

- How do rich people talk about money?

- How do poor people talk about money?

- Practice replacing the negative talk with saying positive things about money (or anything that is negative in your life right now)

LYNDA HYKIN

"Whatever the mind can conceive

and believe,

it can achieve"

-Napoleon Hill

LYNDA HYKIN

SECRET #2

WHAT ARE YOU THINKING?

If I could wave a magic wand and give you any amount of money you want, how much would you want?

$ _____

What would you do with that much money?

List 5 things you would do:

1. _____

2. _____

3. _____

4. _____

5. _____

Sorry, I've lost my magic wand. You can have any amount of money you want, but you will have to earn it for yourself.

Now write down how much money you want:

$ _____

Was the second amount different from the first amount?

What would you change from your first list? What would you cross off or decide not to have?

1. _____

2. _____

3. _____

4. _____

5. _____

Why was the second amount different from the first?

_____

_____

_____

_____

_____

_____

_____

Lesson Number One and how you think about money. If you REALLY wanted what you wrote the first time, the amount shouldn't have changed. It shouldn't have mattered whether I was giving it to you with my magic wand or you had to earn it yourself.

So why did it? Write down 5 reasons why you think you can't have the amount you wrote the first time. Why was it okay if I just gave it to you, but you think you can't have it if you have to earn it yourself?

I can't have $_____ because:

1. _____

2. _____

3. _____

4. _____

5. _____

Knowing you can have whatever it is you want and actually getting whatever it is you want all starts with how you **think** about what you want. You have to develop a different way of thinking than you do now. Just like what you **say** about money – or anything - what you **think** is just as important, perhaps more important.

What you think about is based on what you see, what you hear, what you are taught, and what is repeated over and over. These thoughts eventually become your beliefs. And these beliefs, right or wrong, good or bad, determine how you live your life. You will repeat them over and over because you believe these thoughts are the truth.

Did you know that the average person thinks at least 50,000-60,000 thoughts a day? Can you imagine how strong your belief would be if every day 40,000 of those thoughts were about how you **couldn't** do something?

Let's say you thought red cars were bad, and blue cars were good and you kept thinking this over and over. Eventually you would come to **believe** that red cars are bad. You most likely would never buy a red car. Why would you? You believe they are bad. You can read, hear or see all kinds of different opinions about red cars, that they are good, they are better than blue cars, but deep down inside – you believe they are bad. Something has to happen for you to change your belief; to start thinking and believing differently about red cars or they will always be bad.

People thought and believed the world was flat. People thought and believed man could never reach the moon. People thought and believed it was impossible to fly, or to talk on a phone in a car or on a sidewalk or to see and talk with someone from the other side of the world from the comfort of your own home.

If someone hadn't thought that maybe it could happen, that it was possible, Doctors wouldn't be performing heart and lung transplants or curing diseases. We wouldn't have the technology we have today. We'd still be living in the dark ages!! (OMG! No tweeting, texting, computer, no nothing!)

List 10 people that changed the world because they thought differently from everyone else and made the rest of the world eventually think and believe something different.

   1. Einstein

   2. Henry Ford

   3. _____

   4. _____

   5. _____

   6. _____

   7. _____

   8. _____

   9. _____

 10. _____

Here's a couple more that may not have changed the world like Einstein, but made have made people believe something different and thereby positively impacted hundreds of thousands, even millions of others (clue):

- Tony Robbins
- Oprah Winfrey
- Mother Theresa
- Ghandi

There are lots and lots of 'rags to riches' stories out there, those who have risen from a life of poverty to immense wealth, from enormous failure to incredible success. Why can't you be one of them?

It all starts with how you think and how you speak those thoughts.

You can change your mind any time you want and you can change your beliefs. You have already done that with some beliefs.

List 5 things that you once thought were true, but you don't believe anymore. (Need a couple hints: Tooth fairy/Santa/????)

1. _____
2. _____
3. _____
4. _____
5. _____

So if you now think and believe differently about those things, why can't you think and believe that it's possible for other things, like being successful, rich or whatever you want to be?

You need to create different thoughts in order to create different beliefs. In other words, if you keep thinking you will always be poor – you begin to believe that to be true. But if you change your thoughts and start thinking you could be rich, you will come to believe that THIS is true which by default makes the first belief untrue.

Wealth **is a mindset**. It's about what you think and what you believe.

You have to think it's possible, in spite of your current circumstances, that you are capable of achieving whatever it is you want to achieve; money, career, lifestyle. There is absolutely no reason why you can't have, do, or be anything you want, if you are prepared to work at it, never give up and above all, think and believe it's possible.

Fill in the blanks.

" I used to believe that_____

_____

_____,

but now I believe that _____

_____

_____."

(use words in first blank like; I couldn't/I shouldn't/ I'm not … and in the second blank, words like; I can/ I will/I do/I am.

There is a saying: "What you think about, you bring about." I believe this to be true. I can't possibly believe I am a rock star, if I am always thinking that I will **never** be a rock star, that I'm not good enough, that I can't sing, or play the guitar very well. Even if people keep telling you that you are a great rock star, YOU have to believe it in order for it to be true.

Learn now that other people's opinions are THEIRS, not yours. You can't control what other people think, but you can control what YOU think.

Does this happen over night? Nope. But you can decide right now that you will start to think differently, think positively; about yourself and about your dreams. That it is possible.

Read a book called Making the Impossible Possible, by Bill Strickland. Read about the 8th Grade Millionaire – who was born and lived in unbelievable poverty and by the age of 27 was a millionaire, and by 34 was a billionaire. Read real life rags-to-riches stories. And then tell me that you are any different than they are, that they could do it but you can't.

Creating a new way of living is a 4 step process:

1. What you think
2. What you believe
3. What you say
4. What you do

We've gone over the first 3. Here is number 4, which can drastically change your life for the better.

It's called Habits.

Yep! The various habits you create will become your way of life. You have to choose which habits you want to start, which habits you want to stop and which habits you want to continue and improve.

So what's a habit?

Habits are things you do over and over again,

seemingly without even thinking about them. Breathing would be one of those things. So habits are important, wouldn't you say?

Like everything in life, there are choices. That includes habits. You can develop good habits or bad habits.

Smoking – Bad habit

Exercise – Good habit

List some other habits that you can think of (good or bad)

GOOD HABITS   BAD HABITS

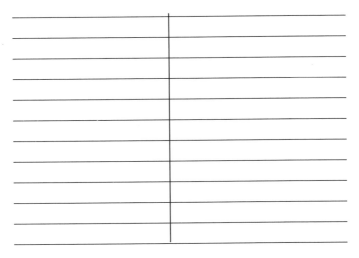

WE develop those habits. They are not pre-programmed into us, we are not born with them. We create them. And we need to create good habits in order to live a good life. Make sense? If you have a bad habit that you have developed, it is possible to change it. And like changing your beliefs, you can change any habit that you have already created.

The first thing to do is recognize the habits that we currently have. Then we have to decide whether they are good habits that we want to keep, or bad habits that we want to change. And then we have to lose the ones we don't want to keep. Can we do that?

Yep.

Here's a scenario to show what I'm talking about:

Every morning you walk into the kitchen and go to the cupboard by the sink for a coffee mug. You know it's there, it's always there. That is a habit – to go to the same spot for the coffee cup. You don't pause and think about where it is – you just know – every morning I go to the cupboard and it's there. That's a habit.

But on the weekend, your Mom rearranged all the cupboards in the kitchen. The coffee mugs are on the other side of the stove. Every day now for the next few days, you start out going to the 'old' spot for the coffee mugs, but they aren't there … and then you remember, 'oh ya', they're over there. It's uncomfortable, and it may even make you grumpy. You may cause a stink and try to put them back where they were, the old way. Eventually, you will go to the new spot without thinking about it. Going to the new spot in the kitchen will become the new habit.

It takes about 30 days to create a new habit. (Which is why the Teenage Money Magnet Project™ is sectioned into 30 day sessions.) If you have a bad habit that you want to stop, don't plan on it happening instantly. Plan on 30 days to imbed the new habit into your brain. Do not beat yourself up if you slip. Simply start again ... and again...and again. Keep starting until it sticks. Because it will eventually stick. It will eventually become the new habit.

When it comes to money, there are also good habits and bad habits. You are so much more fortunate than your parents right now because you have not yet developed too many (or any) bad habits around money. If you follow this book, you will know the difference between good habits and bad when it comes to what you do with your money – and that puts you leagues ahead of adults who have either never learned this, or who have chosen not to change their habits.

Creating good habits now, when there is only a little money involved, will ensure that when you start earning more and more money, those good habits are already well established and you will be able to make the right choices – without even thinking about it. Because you have created those GOOD habits. It doesn't matter how much you have to start with. It only matters that you start.

So what are you thinking – about money, about you, about what you want, and about who you want to be?

What new habits do you want to create?

QUICK SUMMARY:

- What are you thinking? Positive or negative things?
- Thinking the same thing over and over becomes a belief.
- Beliefs are how you live your life.
- Habits are the result of what you think, what you believe and what you repeat over and over.
- List habits you want to:
  - Start
  - Stop
  - Change
  - Improve

"If money be not thy Servant,
it will be thy Master"

- Francis Bacon

LYNDA HYKIN

SECRET #3

DO THE MATH

Okay enough of the self-help blah blah for now. Let's get to some of the good stuff.

We will start off with your new mantra. Before doing anything with your money from now on you will say to yourself:

DO THE MATH.

Repeat this EVERY time you have money and BEFORE you do anything with it: Do the Math. Before you spend, before you make any choices with your money, Do the Math.

Did you know that 90% of the population in Canada is spending 164% of their income.? Anyone here good at math? If you are only making $100, how is it possible to spend $164?

Debt.

Right now, Canadians are seriously in debt. They are spending more than they make. How does this happen?

It's because we want things not now, but RIGHT now! We don't want to wait – for anything. We want the fastest car, computer, phone – the fastest and best everything. And we spend more of our money in order to get it NOW. We pay EXTRA just for that privilege. And others are making millions of dollars off us, because they know we will pay more just to get it now. They get rich, we get debt. Just because we want it NOW!

EXERCISE:

I am going to give you a choice. I will give you a check right now for one million dollars (BTW please don't try to cash it) ... or ... I will give you one cent (I know they don't make pennies anymore, just play along) and I will double it every day for 31 days. Which one do you want? Want the check?

List the first 5 things you are going to do with that money?

   1. _____

How much does it cost? $_____

   2. _____

How much does it cost? $_____

   3. _____

How much does it cost? $_____

   4. _____

How much does it cost? $_____

   5. _____

How much does it cost? _____

     Total Spent on these 5 things:

         $_____

Guess what? Now you have less money than you had just a few short seconds ago. "But", you say, "That's okay…. I still have lots left." (We'll see…)

Did any-one take the penny? Quit snickering – play with me here – someone, take the penny and trust me. Okay, Day 1 you have 1 cent. Day 5 wow – a whole 16 cents. Day 10 and you still only have $5.12. Oh look, day 15 – you have $163.84. Still sucks!

Day #1	$	0.01
2	$	0.02
3	$	0.04
4	$	0.08
5	$	0.16
6	$	0.32
7	$	0.64
8	$	1.28
9	$	2.56
10	$	5.12
11	$	10.24
12	$	20.48
13	$	40.96
14	$	81.92
15	$	163.84

Day 20 earns you $5,242.88. Only 10 days to go, and you're not anywhere close to a million bucks! Okay, I'll let you go right to day 31 –

What happened??

16	$	327.68
17	$	655.36
18	$	1,310.72
19	$	2,621.44
20	**$**	**5,242.88**
21	$	10,485.76
22	$	20,971.52
23	$	41,943.04
24	$	83,886.08
25	$	167,772.16
26	$	335,544.32
27	$	671,088.64
28	$	1,342,177.28
29	$	2,684,354.56
30	$	5,368,709.12
31	**$**	**10,737,418.24**

... and by day 31 that silly, insignificant little penny earned you more than **10 TIMES** what your buddy got by taking the check!

By simply not spending for a short period of time, and doubling your money for just 31 days, you smoked your buddy, who by this time has probably spent most, if not all of his money.

You are probably going to work for 20-30-40 years after you get out of school. (sucks I know ... unless of course you become rich sooner than later because of what you read in this book!) If you put away that silly little penny and doubled it just once a year, in 30 years you would have that same '$10 million plus' amount. Now think about doing this with a dime instead of the penny (add a zero to the bottom number). Now think about $1.00 instead of the dime (add 2 zeros!). Here's where the rich get rich (clue):

Rich people think in years, poor people think in weeks, days or 'right now'.

Start thinking like the rich people. Be patient with your money. Instant gratification is not the way to riches.

You have a choice of becoming rich or poor or 'just getting by'. Once you decide you want to be rich, you have to realize you can't spend it all, or spend more than you make and expect your money to miraculously grow ... or even have any left over.

Do the math:

Earn	$100
Spend	<u>$100</u>
Remaining	0

If you don't learn to change the (bad) habit of spending all you earn, or more than you earn, once you get out into the big wide world of the working, it won't change. While you may make more and more money as time goes on, you will also spend more and more because that's what you have always taught yourself to do.

You are so much luckier (and smarter now) than those adults who don't understand this. It is so much harder to break a bad habit and replace it with a good one – some people never succeed. But you have the opportunity to start the GOOD habit right from the beginning and never develop the bad habit in the first place! The secret to doing this?
That's #4.

QUICK SUMMARY:

This one is easy. Do the Math:

- Before you spend
- Before you make any money decisions
- Create the good habit of patience with money
- Think both short term AND long term
- Know where your money is going, where it went and where it needs to go.

LYNDA HYKIN

"POVERTY HAS MANY ROOTS,

BUT THE TAP ROOT IS IGNORANCE"

- LYNDON B. JOHNSON

LYNDA HYKIN

SECRET #4

SO WHAT DO YOU DO
WITH A DOLLAR?

I learned this from T. Harv Ekker, author of Secrets of the Millionaire Mind. My entire financial future was changed forever (for the better) and I now live my life by the lessons taught in his book and by taking his seminar (several times), The Millionaire Mind Intensive. (yes, BIG clue)

Get 4 jars. Label them as follows:

Jar #1. **Necessities.**

Jar #2. **Freedom**

Jar #3. **Charity**

Jar #4. **Short Term Savings/Spending**

JAR #1: NECESSITIES

Every time you earn a dollar, put 70 cents in this jar. (70% of what you earn.)

This is to be used for necessities **ONLY**. Necessities are things you have to have to live; like food, clothes, rent, etc. Tattoos and body piercings are not a necessity. Clothes are a necessity, but **Designer** clothes are not. And if you believe they are, the money must come out of this jar and nowhere else. Designer clothes cost more money than knock-offs. This means you have less to spend on all the other **necessities**; so less food or cheaper rent. NEVER, EVER spend more than 70 cents on necessities. Starting this habit now will guarantee you will never be poor. If you just do this, take nothing else away from this book, and do nothing else for the rest of your life, you will never be broke. How cool is that?

Oh, BTW – just because you aren't concerned with rent or utilities right now DOES NOT mean you get to spend this 70% somewhere else! SAVE IT. Education can be considered a necessity. If you want to become a Doctor, then University becomes a necessity. This money can be used for that.

The whole point is to start the HABIT of automatically putting 70 cents in this jar **every time** you get a dollar, or 70% of whatever you earn. From now until ... forever.

Once you get out on your own and have your own place, continue to NEVER spend more than 70% of what you earn on necessities. (Rent, bus pass, car insurance/gas/phone/etc) If you earn $2,000 a month, you cannot live in a place that costs $1500 a month – that would leave only $500. That's spending 75% of your money on just rent. You still have to pay for all the other necessities and also into the other jars – do the math; it doesn't add up.

JAR#2 - FREEDOM

Put 10 cents in this jar regardless of anything else going on. (10% of what you earn.)

This is called paying yourself first. You ALWAYS pay yourself first. As soon as you get a dollar – pay yourself first and put the 10 cents in this jar EVERY time. NEVER go even once without putting 10 cents in this jar because this is your Financial Freedom. This is the jar that will make sure you will enjoy freedom from poverty. You can NEVER spend this money. Let me repeat that. You can NEVER spend this money.

Huh?

Yep, that's what I said. It is there to grow and make you even more money. Open up a savings account at a bank and when the jar gets full, put it in your account – and leave it there. This is called the PRINCIPLE amount. The bank will actually **pay you** for doing that! If you leave it in the bank and don't touch it they will give you money for doing that! This is called earning INTEREST. Later, you will use only the INTEREST that you have earned to reinvest and earn even more, but the PRINCIPLE amount is NEVER spent. Yes, it will take time before you have accumulated enough interest to reinvest, and yes, that sucks, but that's the way it is and you have the time.

By never spending the Principle, you will never be broke. You will always have money, because it's this money that will continue to earn you even more. This jar is more than long term, it's lifetime. You can actually pass this down to your children and grand-children. I am not a Financial Planner or an expert in how to make YOUR money grow. That is for you to learn later. (Check out 'Resources the Author Recommends' in the back of the book for some awesome people that have generously donated some of their time so you can contact them about this.)

For now, just learn that you have an account, sitting there, making money – all by itself, without you doing anything!

The only thing I will suggest here, is that you put this money into a Tax Free Savings Account when you turn 18. Right now, it won't matter because you don't have an income high enough to need to know too much about taxes, but eventually you will.

Basically, the Government takes a portion of your income every time you get a paycheck. At the end of the year, if you didn't pay them enough – they take more! I'm sure you've heard adults talking about having to 'do their taxes' in April of every year. Really sucks I know, but that money is what pays for Hospitals, roads, Police etc. (Sometimes you pay too much and the Government gives it back to you.) The benefit of a TFSA account is that you don't have to pay the Government any tax on the **interest** that you earn. This is a good thing!

JAR #3 CHARITY

Always put 10 cents in this jar for Charity, or 'to give back' (10% of what you earn). This is part of the change in thinking you need to establish now. Instead of thinking you will wait until you have lots of money before you start giving, start now. You will feel good, and you will create the mindset that it's okay to give because you believe you will always have more money coming in. This shows that you are grateful for all you have and that you are happy to share with others. Once your jar is full, give it to a Cause you believe in, a Charity or Organization that you think is helping to make a difference in the world. (or start your own foundation or Non-Profit Organization! – more on this later.)

JAR #4   SHORT TERM SAVINGS/SPEND!

So far, you have put away 70 cents for things you HAVE to pay for, 10 cents for your Financial Freedom and 10 cents to Give Back. That leaves 10 cents.

The last 10 cents goes into your short term savings/ SPEND jar. Whoohoo! Finally, money just for you! This is the money you can use for tats or body piercings, I-phones, trips, car or whatever you want to buy. Save up for what you want, then use this money and ONLY this money to get it. Are you addicted to Starbucks?? This is the money you use for that. If you consider life without Starbucks would be pure torture, and this is a necessity – guess where the money has to come from? (Now you understand! You got it!!)

These 4 jars are the only Money Plan you will ever need. Do this for the rest of your life and you will never worry about money again. Do this whenever you get any money, no matter how much or how little. If you get a summer or part time job, do it every time you are paid. Do not EVER miss adding to your jars.

This will give you such an incredible feeling of empowerment, especially when you start to see your money grow! And you CAN do it!

- This is what is going to make you successful.

- This is what is going to make you wealthy.

- This is what is going to guarantee that you will never have to worry about money – ever.

- This is going to make you part of the 3% Club.

What's the 3% Club? Did you know that around 3% of the population earns 97% of the money – in the **world. (and ladies – only 1%of that is owned by us ... but that's another topic).**

If you take every dollar you ever earn, and divide it into these 4 jars, you will belong to the 3% Club.

Imagine! You! Having more wealth than 97% of the population!

Just because of 4 silly jars.

This s the one of the shortest chapters in the entire book. Yet there was really no need to add any more to it, or even to give a Quick Summary.

Just follow the jars.

SECRET #5

PROFITS ARE BETTER
THAN WAGES

So let's earn some money to put in those jars!

How do people earn money?

- _____
- _____
- _____
- _____
- _____

The most common way to earn money is to get a job. Most adults go to work every day for 5 days a week, 8 hours a day. At the end of the week, or every two weeks they get paid. As long as you do the work that is asked of you, you get to keep your job and keep getting paid. If you don't show up, or don't do the work – you no longer have a job and you no longer get paid. If the Company shuts down, goes out of business - you're out of work and your paycheck stops.

Here are 2 examples of a job:

1. McDonald's. They will pay you $10 for every hour that you work. If you work 10 hours in the week you will get $10 X 10 hours = $100. This is what's called earning a **wage.**

2. Suppose you went out into the neighborhood and charged $10 to cut lawns. If you cut 10 lawns you earn the same. 10 lawns X $10 = $100

In these 2 cases, what you are really doing is exchanging your time for money. Can you see any problem here? There are only so many hours in the day that you can work, so there is only so much money that you could make if you give your time in exchange for money.

Yet this is what most people do. They have a job. They work for someone else or a company and earn so much money per hour/week/month.

Who do you think is getting richer? You or the Company? The company is the one that gets richer, not you. When the company makes more money, it goes to the company, not you. Working for a wage simply means they pay you $x no matter what. Every week, you receive the same amount of money. As the Company sell more products or services, they make more money. And you? Nope. You make the same as before.

And that's why profits are better than wages.

What's a profit you ask?

When working at a job, the only way to make more money is to get a raise, ask your boss for more money or quit and work somewhere else that pays more.. You could also gain more skills and move up in the company or change jobs within the company. But you only earn what the Company is willing to pay you, you do not have control of this.

A profit is when you take all the money you earned, subtract your expenses and whatever is left over is profit. In sales, the more you sell – the more you make – the more profit. Profit is unlimited. Wages are not. No matter how much the Company earns in profits – you still make the same wage.

Making a profit sounding better? So here's how to earn a profit:

If you buy a product for $2 and sold it for $3 you would make a **profit** of $1 for every one you sold.

Remember, the profit is the money left over after paying your expenses. In this case your expense is buying the product for $2.

So $3 earned - $2 expenses = $1 profit. Sell 100 and you make $100 profit.

Jim Rohn said that time is more valuable than money. You can get more money but you can't get more time. Why is this important? Let's see.

If you went door to door selling your product, that would take up time. You could perhaps knock on 10 doors in an hour and sell 10 items. But that same hour of work can earn **different** amounts of money, depending on the **quantity** of products you sell at **each** house. If you sold 1 to 1 house, you made $10. Sell 4 to 1 house, you made $40 in the same amount of time. If you sell 30 to 30 people, you make $300. Sell 30 to 10 people – less time, same money.

Now it's not the **TIME** that you are being paid for, but the number of products you sell. The better you are at selling them, the more products you sell, the more money you make. What if you set up a website and sold your product online? You could sell while you were sleeping! Thousands of people thousands of miles away could simply click and buy your product - at the same time. And that's just **one** business.

Now, let's really go crazy – what if you had more than one business? What if you had thousands of products? Ding ding!!

And **that's** why making a profit is better than earning a wage. Because meanwhile, back at the Company, you are still getting the same pay and depending on the boss, the owner of the Company, to keep giving it to you, depending on them to not go out of business or close up shop, and to responsibly manage *their* money so they will have some to give to you on pay day.

In reality, earning a profit is not as simple as above. It requires hard work, having a product that people actually want to buy and a lot of other factors. The point I'm making is to start thinking about other ways to earn money besides a 'job'. Realize there are options out there.

Yes, Doctors, Lawyers, Corporate Executives earn oodles of money, but they STILL earn a wage. Somebody else is paying them. If the Company closes – their job is gone. Even if you owned your own Practice in Medicine or Law, you could only see so many patients or clients per day.

Now you have an advantage; knowing that you can earn money by other (legal) means; by earning a profit and not just by earning a wage.

And guess what?

You can do both! At the same time! Yep! You can be a Corporate Executive, a Doctor, a Lawyer, and make a profit doing something else while your practicing your profession! Sweet! This is called Multiple Streams of Income. And if you want, you can have as many streams of income as you want!

I used to bounce from job to job. I would get all excited about something, and then find out it wasn't as great as I thought, so I would move on. People called me flighty. They said I never 'stuck' to anything. That I was always running around trying new things when I should be sticking my nose to the grind stone. (sorry, old fashioned expression there.) I give thanks EVERY DAY that I didn't follow their 'advice' to stay put!

Today more and more people are realizing that they can have more than one business, they can earn money from doing more than one thing. I have see many business cards with two companies on it. I have met people that have handed me several of their business cards, not just one. Personally I have 4 cards at the moment.

Don't confuse this with 'working 2 jobs'. When I suggest to people about having another source of income, they automatically assume I mean a second 'job'.

Remember, there are only so many hours in the day that you can work. Having 2 jobs is not the same as having a second (or third or fourth or twentieth) source of income. I don't want to complicate things too much, but here are some 'alternate' sources of earning a profit as opposed to earning a wage:

Home-based /business – Start a business from home. You are your own boss. This is usually a part-time thing to start off with, while you are earning a wage somewhere else. An example of home-based business would be catering out of your kitchen, or accounting. Multi-level Marketing is usually a home-based business, such as selling Avon, Arbonne or Organo Gold.

Residual Income – An example of residual income would be reorders on products that occur automatically. You sell the customer a product one time, then they reorder over and over again automatically, without you having to resell to them.

Online/internet business - Millions have been made on the internet. The benefit is that it is global – people from all over the world can buy your product.

Referrals – You simply refer someone (company or product) and if someone buys the product, the person/company you referred pays you a predetermined sum.

Passive Income

I saved this for last. This is the one that no-one teaches you about. There is no course in high school, college or any university titled Passive Income 101. Yet this is the game changer. This is the difference between being rich and wealthy, or being broke and living pay cheque to pay cheque.

What is passive income?

Passive income is an income received on a regular basis, with little or no effort required to maintain it. It is money you earn even when you aren't actively working the business.

Here is the **'work less, get paid more'** part.

Ah! I see I have your attention! Wow, you even put the phone down! Smart move. This is important. Learning about passive income will have you making money over and over again.

The average person earns an income that stops coming in when they stop working. If you get paid a salary and you quit your job or get laid off, you'll stop getting paid. Your boss won't keep paying your salary unless you keep showing up for work.

If you are in a service industry (like a physical therapist) and have clients who pay you directly or you are self employed and your customers/clients stop coming - you stop getting paid. If you don't show up for work, again, you don't get paid. With passive income, you keep getting paid whether or not you do any meaningful work in the business.

WAIT! Of course it's not that easy!

You must do a lot of work up front to get the ball rolling, but eventually you reach a point where the passive income stream gets activated. At this point you can essentially stop working on this income stream if you want, and money will continue to keep flowing in regardless of whether you do anything or not.

Aren't you glad you picked up (were forced to read) this book? There is truly a magic genie! And his name is Passive Income. This is how the rich get rich, how the wealthy continue to become wealthier. And this is what so few people know about, or are willing to get out of their comfort zone to do. And this is why 97% of the population is working for someone else, or are living paycheck to paycheck.

Excited to learn more? Thought so. Imagine! While you're sitting on a beach somewhere chillin', money is going into your bank account without you doing anything! Now THAT's what I call a job!

Some examples of passive income are:

- You own a store or business, but have others work and manage it.

- Rental income from investment properties

- Coin operated machines – such as vending machines, laundry mats

- Parking lots – People pay you to park there, automatically – they simply swipe their credit card and the money goes directly into your account. Some older lots still have meters or an attendant. Anyway you do it, you don't have to be there to earn an income

- Royalties - from publishing a book, licensing a patent or other forms of intellectual property, such as computer software products. Music, movies and screenplays also earn royalties and can be very lucrative

- Earnings from internet advertisements on websites - If you own a website people will pay you for the privilege of advertising their business on it. Every time someone clicks and buys something from the link on your site – you get paid.

Sounds great, right? (Of COURSE there's a catch!) Passive income does NOT work for the lazy types who spend 12 hours a day playing Angry Farm Ninja Madness. Nor is it intended for the desperate "I need to make $500 by Friday to pay my rent" types. Creating passive income is work. Like everything in life, first you do the work, then you reap the rewards.

Remember, here is the 'cha ching!' You can have **as many** passive income streams as you **want**! It is limited only by your imagination. You may have heard the expression, 'never put all your eggs in one basket'? Well, don't just limit yourself to 'one source of income'. Having **multiple sources of income** is one of the shortest, fastest, best ways to achieving wealth, to becoming financially free, to living the lifestyle you desire.

$11.00 per hour is not.

Just as long as you follow the 'jars'.

LYNDA HYKIN

QUICK SUMMARY:

- Profits are better than wages.

- You can get more money, but you can't get more time

- Having multiple streams of income is the shortest, quickest, best way to achieving wealth

- Research all kinds of different ways to earn an income other than just a job (working for someone else)

- Start thinking about your own 'multiple streams of income'

LYNDA HYKIN

"Do what you fear

and the death of fear

is certain"

- Anthony Robbins

LYNDA HYKIN

SECRET #6

BREAKING THE POVERTY CYCLE

When you are in the Poverty Cycle, you receive an income, you spend it, your broke. Your self esteem goes down. You feel worthless, frustrated. You don't see how to get out of it…because there is not enough money to go around. You think you need more money to fix it. You may get more money but it still doesn't get fixed.

THE POVERTY CYCLE

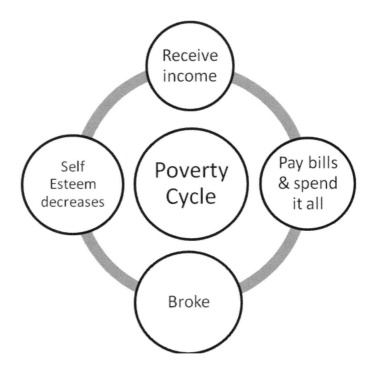

Who started this cycle anyway?

Who cares.

Everybody has a story. Some have a story of poverty, sickness, drugs or alcohol, physical, sexual or mental abuse. Others have a story of health and happiness and love.

It doesn't matter. Jack Canfield, Author of "Chicken Soup for the Soul" series and The Success Principles", says that's just called, "So what?" The real 'what' is, "What are you going to do about it now?"

All that matters is that you want to go from living in the Poverty Cycle to living in the Wealth Cycle.

THE WEALTH CYCLE

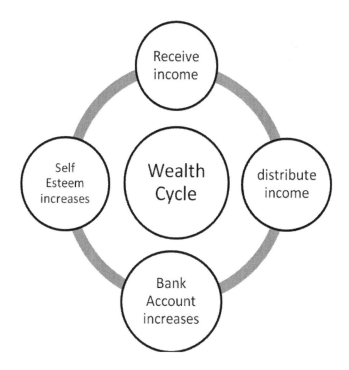

When you are in the Wealth Cycle, you receive an income, you divide it into your 4 jars. All your expenses are covered, your financial future is secured. You have learned to make your money work for you, and you are able to save for something you want.

Every time you complete this cycle (like every payday), your self esteem goes up. You are more confident. You believe in yourself and you know that you can have, be and do whatever you want – because you have proven it by completing the cycle. So how do you get from one cycle to the other? First, take the **DOWN** Stairs.

Unlike 'climbing UP to success' when it comes to fear you have to go DOWN not up … into the deep, dark, scary basement of your mind. Spooky! Your mind will talk you out of anything if you let it and most of the time it is successful, and most of the time it is because deep down inside –

You are afraid:

1. Of failure

2. Of ridicule

3. Of being different

4. Of not being worthy of having what you want

5. Of being undeserving

6. Of success – Yes, people are actually afraid of success. Because with success comes responsibility; of maintaining and managing the success. Otherwise…..failure (see #1)

There are many other reasons why, but fear stops most of us. And you can't ignore it because it doesn't go away. You'll just push it further and further down into your sub-conscious mind, where it will lay in wait for you.

You cannot overcome fear unless you acknowledge it, that you admit to yourself that it exists. So first up, it's okay to be afraid. It does not make you weak. You cannot ignore it and pretend it's not there. Because it is. What you *do* have to do is deal with it. Find out where it is coming from and then face it.

Think of a dark and spooky basement. You hear noises coming from there. You could stand at the top of the stairs and be afraid of all the creepy, freaky things that might be making that noise. You can conjure up boogey men, fierce and vicious gargoyles, ghosts or goblins. You can be very afraid to go down into that basement for fear – of what you DON'T know. You can choose to NEVER go down there, to run away, or to make your little sister go down there first.

Or

You can turn your back on the fear. Arm yourself, turn on the light and take it step by step until you are there, until you check everything out and find the source of the noise. Once you do, the fear leaves. You can go down into the basement anytime now without fear. You acknowledged that you were afraid, and then you went and found out what it was that you were afraid of. You do the same thing with the fear that comes up when you are going for your dreams.

There is a difference between realistic fear, and UN-realistic fear. If you don't study, don't take notes, don't show up or listen in class, and you know there is a test coming up, you most likely will worry (be afraid) that you won't pass. That is realistic.

The obvious way to confront that fear and overcome it, is to listen in class, study, ask for extra help if you need it.

But if you pay attention in class, study hard, get the extra help and STILL worry, (are afraid) that you won't pass, this is UN-realistic and you may want to ask yourself why you are afraid of not passing.

"I probably won't pass 'cause the Teacher hates me." Why do you think that? It isn't that you're afraid you won't pass, it's a problem with the Teacher that needs solving.

See where I'm going here? Think of fears as just problems that need solving.

So what are you afraid of? When it comes to money or anything that you don't believe you can achieve or overcome, what is it that you are REALLY afraid of?

I worry that (I'm afraid that):

_____

_____

_____

_____

_____

_____

_____

_____

_____

There is a beautiful park that I went running through every morning when I was living in Richmond BC. On one run the first week of May, I saw a Mama duck with a whole whack of babies waddling down to the pond. Honestly, there must have been 15 or 20 babies! When they got to the pond, Mama went right into the water. One brave little one followed right behind. The rest stayed at the top and squawked, but didn't venture any further. Mama ignored them. I wanted to get a closer look and as I approached the babies, an interesting thing happened. About half the babies saw me coming, and waddled as fast as they could, down into the water and to the safety of Mama. But a few stayed still or hopped around, sensing danger but not knowing what to do about it.

The next day; same Mama, same babies (I'm guessing). This time when Mama went into the water she was followed by most of the babies. Still a few hung back until I approached. Then they too went in. Only one or two STILL didn't follow.

The babies were afraid to follow Mama into the water. But when a bigger fear came along (me), they chose to jump into the water, to brave the 1st fear. The second time they went into the water, it was easier for them. They weren't afraid because they had already done it once. It didn't take long before they were all waddling down by themselves without a second thought about being afraid. The fear was gone.

In the beginning, they had decided that there was a bigger fear than the water – me. They chose to conquer the smaller fear – the water. They figured out that the water was in fact nothing to fear and that by being in the water, they were actually safe – because I couldn't reach them.

Fears are just things we worry about happening … in the future. They haven't actually happened, but we think they might. What if it all goes wrong? What if I can't do it? But you don't know 100% for a fact that it will happen.

So why can't you think that it won't happen? Why can't you think that you are capable of finding a solution to the problem? Why can't you think that it might all go right?

Take your top 3 fears about money and write them down.

1._____

_____

2._____

_____

3._____

_____

How would you feel if you were no longer afraid?

_____

_____

_____

_____

_____

What is the worst thing that could happen if you confronted the fear?

_____

_____

_____

_____

What is the best thing that could happen if you confronted the fear?

_____

_____

_____

_____

_____

NOTE:

I am not talking here about physical violence or bullying or abuse of any kind. If that is happening in your life you need to tell someone, get help NOW. There are all kinds of places to go for help.

I am talking about making choices based on your fear. If you are afraid to stand up in front of the class and give a speech, you limit yourself from endless possibilities. I chose this one on purpose. Did you know that more people are afraid of public speaking than death?

Corporate Executives have to stand up in front of clients or employees and talk and give presentations. But I'll bet most of them were afraid to do it when they first started. Some may even still be afraid of getting up in front of people to speak. I can almost guarantee that if they had decided not to face this fear, they would not hold the position of an Executive that they do. It's a part of their job.

There is help out there for facing almost any fear and public speaking has a great support group - Toastmasters International. It is a global Organization where you can practice speaking in a safe and friendly environment. Many great Speakers have come from a start in one of the Clubs that are around the world. Check it out if that is one of your fears.

ANOTHER NOTE:

In the back of this book is a list of Canadian Resources for Teens for all different kinds of support: drugs/alcohol/homelessness/poverty/abuse/bullying/self esteem/language barriers/ etc

Please make use of this if you have ANYTHING going on in your life that you need help with.

Again, it's ok to be afraid. Recognize that you are, and then take the stairs down and down and down, until you figure out what it is that you're really afraid of and then confront it.

And then go do it anyway.

You can also break the Poverty Cycle by remembering this sentence:

How you do **ANY**thing is how you do **EVERY**thing.

You get to create your own core values. Core values are statements about who you want to be with respect to how you live your life. Do you want to be someone who is ethical? Professional? Sincere? Honest? These are core values. Long after tats have become no longer cool (although the tat remains for *ever*) or the giant sized hole in the earlobes have caused safety or health issues, your core values remain. Broke or wealthy, they will remain the same unless you change them or create new ones. Another word for your core values would be Standards. Think of it as setting the Standards of your life.

You have the opportunity to develop your core values now, without having to retrain yourself like older people would. You get to start fresh. And those core values are based on this:

How you do **any**thing is how you will do **every**thing.

When you go to do or say something – it will be a reflection of how you do or say everything else in your life. Cheating on a test will find you cheating at other things or on other people. Helping someone for no personal gain will find you helping in other areas, and perhaps making a huge, positive impact on something or someone. Every time you go to do something, remember this sentence. If you want to quit, cut corners, lie, or not do your best, it will show up when you do other things. It will become a habit. Eventually, it will become your life and how you live your life. So how you do anything is how you do everything. Establish your core values now. They will change along the way, as you change. But establish what you want right now. Use the word 'MUST'. This is not a 'nice-to-say' thing. These core values are going to shape the man or woman you will become. They come from the heart and from the gut. They become who you **are.**

Here are mine if it helps you get started.

1. I must be of service to others

2. I must do my best

3. I must love what I do

4. I must give generously and receive openly

5. I must make an impact

Write down 3-5 of your Core Values

1. I must _____

2. I must _____

3. I must _____

4. I must _____

5. I must _____

"Great. I have Core Values. Well, whoop-dee-doo! What good are they? Where do I DO with them?"

If you ever read Alice in Wonderland, when asked by the rabbit, "Where do you want to go?" She replied, "I really don't much care." "Then, said the rabbit, "It really doesn't matter how you get there."

If you don't know where you want to go, then how will you know when you've arrived? What good is being totally AWESOME if you don't know what to do with it?

You have to know where you want to go and who you want to be.

You have to have a plan.

LYNDA HYKIN

QUICK SUMMARY:

- Break the Poverty Cycle
- Start the Wealth Cycle
- Your 'story' starts now, no matter what has happened before
- Understand that it is okay to be afraid.
- Acknowledge your fear
- Face your fear
- Do it anyway
- Set your Core Values

LYNDA HYKIN

SECRET #7

THE PLAN

True Story

Two ladies turned 80 years old. One decided that she had best put her affairs in order because she would probably not be around much longer. The other decided that she would like to climb a mountain.

At the age of 93, Huda Crooks became the oldest woman ever to climb Mount Fuji in Japan.

The Stair Steps to creating a Plan

STEP # 1 - DECIDE

- What you want
- Why you want it
- When do you want by?

WHAT

Make a decision about what you want to do, have or be. That may sound strange but you would be surprised how many people don't know what they want. Some adults in their 40's and 50's when asked that question still don't know. Also decide if it's just something that you would like, or something that you REALLY want. If you REALLY want it, you will do whatever it takes to achieve it (legally, please). If not, you won't work hard to accomplish it – and you most likely won't ever get it.

Now, WHY do you want it? The 'Why' is just as important as the 'What'. If you don't have a strong enough reason to work hard to get what you want, then at the first sign of failure, you'll quit. The first time it gets hard, you'll stop. The first time someone says you can't do it, you'll believe them.

Your reason - your "Why" is personal to you and you don't even have to tell anyone what it is. My 'why' to quit smoking was my unborn Grandson. I didn't want him to remember his Nana as the 'stinky cigarette smelling lady'. Once I found that 'why', there was nothing that was going to stop me from quitting. (That was 6 years ago, yay me!)

You just have to believe in it. It may even be, "I'm going to do this, just to show them I'm not a failure!" (This attitude will change, but if that's all you've got to go on at the beginning, use it.)

Make your 'Why' profound. The Bigger the 'Why' and the more important it is to you, the better chance you will have at succeeding.

It's as simple as writing down this statement:

I want _____ because

_____

_____

_____.

WHEN Do you want it? (and don't say, "NOW", lol

Set a time-frame. Like an appointment, you can't just show up whenever **you** want; you are given a certain time to be there. Your Plan also needs to have a time frame. "Someday" translates into 'never'. Even if it is just, 'By the time I'm 25, I want to have/do/be…" This is called setting goals. "What by when", is a sentence to repeat whenever you are setting a goal. Decide what you want, why you want it, and when you want to accomplish it.

I want _____ by
_____because
_____
_____
_____.

Repeat as required for each goal that you set.

#2 – TAKE ACTION

Question: Three frogs are sitting on a lily pad. One decides to jump off. How many are left? You say 2?

Nope!

The frog only **decided** to jump, he didn't actually **do** it.

You can think about, day dream, and talk all you want about what you want; to be successful, rich, or whatever. You can decide you are going to do it. Yep! I'm going in! I'm doing it! But the frog didn't do anything but 'decide'. He will never leave the lily pad – until he jumps. And it's the same with most people.

Most people have 'When' dreams:

- When I grow up,

- When I have a job,

- When I'm rich,

- When …When… When …

A 'when' dream is like wishful thinking. It would be nice, that would be fun, maybe someday. You have no intention of actually doing anything about making it happen, making it a reality. Making a decision is only the first step in making what you want a reality.

Deciding is a great first step, but it will go nowhere on its own. You must take Action.

Acting on your decision – right now, with what you have from where you are must take place. If you want to lose weight but you never get off the couch and keep stuffing chips and pizza and pop into your mouth, it won't happen. If you want to learn a second language, but never pick up a book, take lessons or have someone teach you, it will never happen.

Write out your Plan in your notebook. Just the act of putting it down in writing, makes it more real. You can **feel** the change in your thinking, you can **feel** the excitement, and you will begin to believe it's possible.

This may seem silly I know, but just do it. It's not like you have to show it to anyone. Then read it - every day. Once in the morning and once just before going to bed.

Now, unlike fear, this time we are going to go **UP** stairs, not down. We are going to use The Stair Step Strategy and go UP to your goal/your dream. This was taught to me by a woman who is a brilliant serial entrepreneur. I now use this approach in ALL areas of my life and it works.

Here's the reason it works. Quite simple really. If you can't accomplish small goals or knock off the small steps, how on earth do you plan to achieve the really big ones? You want to be a rock star. You can't simply walk out your door and poof! you're a rock star. You CAN eat an elephant – but not in one bite. You need a plan – a strategy. Then you need action steps to achieve it.

Let's say you want a car. Start at the bottom.

Step One

What kind of car you want? Think about it right down to the small details. What make, model, style and color is it? Is it new or used? What color is the interior? What year is it? How much does it cost? Find a picture of it and post it on your wall, laptop, phone, bathroom mirror, on your ceiling in your room – somewhere

where you will see it every day. See yourself having it, driving it, cruising down the road with the windows open in it every day.

Step Two

Why do you want it? Always ask why – this is what will keep you going when you want to quit, when it gets hard, when you feel like you will **never** get it.

Step Three

When do you want it by? Set a time frame. It should be a realistic time frame. "I want a thousand dollars by Friday", is most likely not happening. Time frames encourage you to keep working on your goal. If you have no idea when you want it by, you most likely will keep putting off doing anything to achieve it. "I want to have my own car by my 18th birthday" is realistic – if you are 16 now. Remember to start at the **BOTTOM.**

Step Four:

What can you do today, right now, to set this in motion? Perhaps the first thing would be to discuss it with your parents. Make a list of everything that goes along with owning a vehicle; insurance, money for gas, license plates, etc. Let them know that you have thought of what owning a car involves, and that you have a plan on how to get it. The lesson here is if you can't knock off phase one, if you can't complete the first steps toward your goal, how are you going to complete the BIGGER steps required?

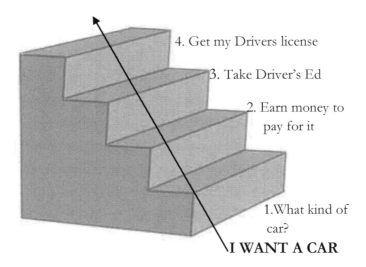

4. Get my Drivers license

3. Take Driver's Ed

2. Earn money to pay for it

1.What kind of car?

I WANT A CAR

Action: This could be actually getting a job or earning money to pay for all that will be needed. What kind of a job, how many hours a week can you work without interfering with your school work, home work, soccer or music?

(Clue) If you are looking for part time work, look in a field that you might actually want to work at FULL time when you are starting a career.

T. Harv Ekker tells the story of wanting to own a Bakery, so he got a job working in one, sweeping floors, and then being promoted to cashier. What he found out very quickly was he absolutely HATED working in the Bakery, and still can't even look at a pie! Better to have found out then, rather that dump tons of money into a business! There is nothing wrong with trying something and finding out it is not meant for you, that you don't like it. What IS wrong is never trying it in the first place (more on this later).

I break each goal into 'stair steps' for a reason. If you had one thousand steps between you and your goal, or if each step were 10 feet tall, it would be overwhelming, you wouldn't believe you could achieve it, it would appear too big and you would most likely quit. So break it down. Make sets of smaller 'stair steps' until you prove to yourself that you can accomplish them and gain the confidence to tackle the bigger ones.

If you want to drive a car from Toronto to California, you do not need to see the entire road. You only need to see the next 200 feet or so. You DO need a map, or a GPS. It would be a good idea to know how long it will take you, so you can plan the number of stop-overs and the best places to spend the night. That's what the plan is for. But you don't need to be able to physically SEE from Toronto to California.

And you don't need to SEE your entire path, you just need to start and go step by step.

The **end result** of breaking down your big goal into steps to achieve them is this:

YOUR VERY OWN CAR!!!!

The bonus to creating The Plan: Inspired Ideas

Every day, you use or see thousands of products, services and systems. You see billboards, TV commercials, magazine ads everywhere promoting something. Those are someone's inspired ideas. Have you ever been using an item and thought of a way to improve it? Or used it for a purpose that it was not intended for? What did you do about that idea? Did you suddenly find your idea on the shelves in stores? How did that make you feel? "Hey, that was MY idea!!" Did you think, "It's too simple" or "someone's probably already thought about it so I there is no sense doing anything?".

An idea is only a thought without form until you set a goal, make a plan to achieve that goal and put that plan into action. Don't' dismiss any inspired idea at least until you have investigated it! Write them down before you forget them. Has someone already done that? Is there a better way to do it? Can you make any money doing it? Inspired ideas get you excited about possibilities. Don't discount them until you have done some research.

MANY of my inspired ideas have gone nowhere. MANY of my ideas have gone nowhere but led me to somewhere else. This book is one of those.

If you have an idea about something - go with it to see where it leads. It may not go anywhere, may lead you to somewhere else completely different, or it may turn out to be a phenomenal experience! Either way, you will learn from it, you will learn to trust yourself, you will learn to take some calculated risks and you will learn to create a plan and to take the 'stairs' one at a time to go after it.

LYNDA HYKIN

QUICK SUMMARY:

- You know what you want, why you want it and when you want it by.
- You have created the stair step approach to achieve what you want and you start NOW to do whatever you can
- You never quit
- You believe that you can and that you will achieve whatever it is you want
- You pay attention to inspired ideas

I can guarantee that your dreams will change, that what you want now will most likely change later as you get older and gain new experiences. Doesn't matter. Right now, this is what you want. Decide you want it and then start doing something about it, whatever it is. If what you want changes along the way, that's okay. You have at least created the habit of making decisions and acting on them, of developing The Plan.

LYNDA HYKIN

"We make a living by what we get.

We make a life by what we give."

- Sir Winston Churchill

LYNDA HYKIN

SECRET #8

THE GRATITUDE ATTITUDE
and
GIVING BACK

"Fame or integrity, which is more important? Money or happiness, which is more valuable? Success or failure, which is more destructive? If you look to others for fulfillment you will never truly be fulfilled. If your happiness depends on money, you will never be happy with yourself. Be content with what you have; rejoice in the way things are. When you realize there is nothing lacking, the whole world belongs to you."

-Lao-tzu

You woke up this morning. You had a roof over your head, and (hopefully) food in your tummy. You have eyes to read this, or ears to listen to an audio version. Be grateful.

I know, I know! I used to hear all the time from my mother about how I should eat those nasty lima beans glaring at me from my plate. There were children starving in other countries, I should be grateful I have food at all!

BTW, my suggestion to send them my lima beans did NOT go over well and I lived in the days of corporal punishment for talking back!

But my Mom was right in a way. We should be grateful for what we have – right now. You may not have a bedroom in a 20 room mansion, but you have a bedroom. You don't drive a Porsche or get driven to school in a limo, but you get to go to school. (Yes, that is a good thing.) You live in a country that allows you free will. My whole point is that you need to feel grateful for what you have now, no matter how little or how much that is.

Scientifically, it has been proven that the more you are truly grateful, the happier and healthier you are. Being grateful for things in your life will affect your personality, your career, your health, your emotional state and even improve your social life. (There you go, no other reason needed!) In the opposite scenario, the more ungrateful, the more you focus on what you don't have, the more unhappy and frustrated you will be. The poor-little-me syndrome will just make you sadder. (and poorer … is that a word?)

In the movie, "The Secret" by Rhonda Byrne, there is a man by the name of Lee Brower who is a Wealth Planner and Entrepreneur. In the movie, he talks about his 'gratitude rocks'. He basically picks up a couple rocks; plain, ordinary rocks, and puts them in his pocket. Whenever he touches them, it reminds him to be grateful. I really liked this idea. I am always picking up one or two little rocks and carrying them around in my hand when I go for a walk. I'm probably going to be remembered as the crazy lady with a huge kick-ass rock collection! You will find them all over my house! Plain, ordinary rocks, but they have an amazing affect on me. If I'm frustrated or angry or having a bad day, I just need to pick up a couple or even just look at them and they remind me to think of GOOD things that happened that day and to feel grateful for what I have.

It's all about recognizing the good things that are going on in your life right now, and taking the focus away from the bad things, or things you don't like. I am not telling you to walk around all day long, pretending that everything is perfect. The world is not perfect and no-one in the world is perfect.

It's just about realizing that when you focus on positive, good things, you begin to see more positive, good things, and more positive, good things start happening to you.

I'm not going to ask you to go out and start collecting rocks but what you can do is start writing down 3 things that you are grateful for EVERY day in your notebook. I have been doing this for about 4 years now. First thing in the morning, I write down all the good things that happened the day before. It sets a positive tone for my day. Others prefer to do it just before they go to bed at night so they end the day on a positive note. Either way works. I call it my Success Journal.

Some days I write a whole page, some days the only thing I can come up with is that I brushed my teeth; it doesn't matter. It has to be more than 2 things and it has to be something positive; a success, something you are grateful you did, or had happen, or something that didn't happen. They can be things like, 'I passed my Math Test' or "I met this great person". Even challenges that you faced are a success. DO THIS EVERY DAY. *Watch what happens in just a very short period of time!*

You will begin to see the world differently, with more good in it than bad. You will start to have a more positive outlook about many things, including yourself and your life and the people around you. Self image, self esteem and self confidence will begin to improve.

People want to hang out with fun, happy people. It's another cycle –

So, what does this have to do with money? Lots. Ever had a really nasty, grumpy, sales person? Did it make you want to spend even more money shopping in that store, just so you could be treated with disrespect or ignored or made to feel like a nobody? Of course not. You may even leave the store without buying anything! Good for your bank account, but not good for the store's.

People don't want to part with their money unless they have a good experience in return for doing so. You trust people that are positive more than those who are negative and you are more willing to part with your hard-earned cash to those that make you feel good. A positive, grateful attitude will have people engaged with you, listening to you and trusting you. They will be willing to part with their money more freely. If you're in Sales, what do you think this would mean?

People also want to hang around happy, positive, successful people. They will want to hang out with you. They will want to help you. They will want to offer you opportunities (opportunity = money). I left a car lot one time when shopping for a car because of the Salesperson's attitude. I wouldn't work with a certain real estate agent when buying a house, just because of the negativity that they projected. In both these cases they lost money – a lot of money. They were on commission so, no sale, no money.

The more you appreciate things, the more people appreciate you.
The more you are grateful for things, the more you are shown   gratitude. And having a 'Gratitude Attitude'

will attract more things to be grateful for.

Then you can go out and show others the way they can begin to catch the 'Gratitude Attitude'.

And you do this by giving back.

Remember your jars? There was one there for Giving. Here is something really cool. You don't need to just give money – you can give – you.

The hardest part for people to get sometimes is to give **first**, then get. But the best way to receive is by giving! You can insert "The Gratitude Cycle" here. Giving works the same way. Give/feel good/ good things start to happen/you want to give more!

Jim Rohn is one of the greatest philosophers I have ever had the honor to connect with through his seminars and speeches. (BIG clue here folks).

Jim said, **"Find a way to serve the many, for service to many leads to greatness."**
Zig Ziglar, another great 'person clue' said, *"If you help enough people get what they want, you can have everything you want"*.

These 2 may be old timers and they are no longer with us, but their wisdom and their message is still totally relevant today and I highly recommend you check them out.

If you want to be great, help others be great. If you want to have more money, help others get more money and then you will have more than you need.

"Ya, but I'm only 15, what can I give?" Well, you can volunteer. Figure out something you love to do or a cause that you feel very strongly about and then volunteer some of your time. This is also a great addition to your resume when you do start looking for a job.

- Like to read? The libraries are always looking for people to read to others.
- Got serious talent playing an instrument? Teach others how to play.
- Start a Charity or Non Profit … and don't say you are too young to do this. Check out www.ladybugfoundation.ca (that's homework, I'm not going to tell you any more)
- Share your skills and talents with others. You can create online 'how to' videos or podcasts
  - Be an Advocate for those who can't speak or do for themselves.

You are only limited by your imagination.

There is always a way to give back. Make this a part of your life. Getting the Gratitude Attitude and Giving back.

Try it for the next 90 days and see what happens. You will be blown away. Trust me.

QUICK SUMMARY:

- Be grateful for what you have now
- The more you give, the more you receive
- Share your Gratitude Attitude with others
- Volunteer – doing something you love to do

LYNDA HYKIN

Becoming a Teenage

Money Magnet™

LYNDA HYKIN

"You aren't wealthy until you have something money can't buy."

- Garth Brooks

LYNDA HYKIN

.

SECRET #9

BE RICH OR BE WEALTHY?

What's the difference between being rich and being wealthy? No they're not quite the same thing.

You could earn a million dollars a year, which makes you rich, but if you spent it all, you would not be wealthy.

Justin Bieber earned $53 million in 2012. Miley Cyrus earned only $46 million. (Only??)

HOWEVER:

Justin Bieber is WORTH $**130** million, while Miley is WORTH $**150** million.
Miley earned less than Justin, yet Miley is worth **more**

because she has invested her money differently, to make even more money. If both Miley and Justin cashed in everything they owned, Miley wins.

What you're Worth = Wealth.
What you Earn = Rich.

This is simple: Poor people want to be rich. Rich people want to be wealthy. What do you want to be?

Rich people have money. Wealthy people have assets. Rich is waking up at 4am in the middle of winter in order to take the long trip by Go train to make millions at your job. Wealthy is waking up when you want.

A person who is rich is someone who has accumulated a lot of money in the bank. And rich to you may mean something different than what rich means to someone else. $1,000,000 to you may mean you're rich. To Donald Trump, it's a drop in the bucket and he would probably feel like he was broke.

Robert Kiyosaki wrote a book called "Rich Dad, Poor Dad" (clue). This book by the way, has made many thousands of people very wealthy. (Just sayin'.)

Anyway, in it he says that the definition of wealth is the number of days you can survive without physically working (or anyone in your household physically working) and still maintain your standard of living. For example, if your monthly expenses are $5,000 and you have $20,000 in savings, your wealth is approximately four months or 120 days. Wealth is measured in time, not dollars. The rich on the other hand, might have lots of money but they also might have lots of expenses. (there's that 'debt' word again.) Or they might have a high paying job but they have to get up to go to work every day to earn that money.

A person who is wealthy is someone who has enough money to guarantee themselves any lifestyle they choose regardless of any poor decisions they make around it; someone who no longer needs to make money. In other words, if they blew a whole whack of money on the stock market, they would still have enough to continue their way of living.

Ants have wealth. But they are not rich.

So the difference in simple terms is 'rich' is what you earn, wealth is what you have. And wealthy is better than rich.

And the way to becoming wealthy is to understand that wealth is a mindset. It's about what you do, not what you have. Wealthy people are not just rich in the bank account, but in the mind as well. They have a significant impact on the lives of many people. You can tell the difference between a wealthy person and a rich person pretty easily. Most wealthy people don't stand out as much as the rich people. While the rich may flaunt their money with fancy cars, houses, and toys, the wealthy tend to live quieter but still adventurous lives. Rich people are motivated by money but wealthy people are motivated by their dreams, purpose and passion. They do what they do to make their life more fulfilling and others lives more interesting, not because they can't wait to drive that new sports car.

Our modern day world is obsessed with money for all the wrong reasons. We look at it as a gateway for solving all of our problems but any wealthy person will tell you that more money equals more problems and more responsibility to handle those problems and that it takes a person that has been through the challenges to reach success to handle them. Again, Robert Kiyosaki says, "It's not how much money you make that matters but how much money you keep—and how long that money works for you."

So becoming wealthy is something to strive for far more than just becoming rich. And wealth can be measured in more than just dollars. Spiritually and mentally you can be very wealthy. Remember, it's a mindset.

What being rich or having wealth means to you is totally different than to someone else. It is personal and it only has importance to you. Go after the wealth that YOU want, not what you think it should be, or how much others think it should be. Don't attach a dollar value to it.

Whether you decide that you want to work 9-5 in a regular job, have a part time business on the side, or work 'outside the career' box in a business or profession that doesn't conform to the 'norm', you can be rich or wealthy doing any of those things. Owning your own business, earning a living as a doctor or lawyer or missionary, create the wealth that surrounds what you love to do.

I have the most amazing grandchildren.

This makes me VERY wealthy!

LYNDA HYKIN

"Whether you think you can

or think you can't

you're right."

- Henry Ford

LYNDA HYKIN

SECRET #10

YOUR FUTURE IS BLANK

Today I woke up and_____

_____

_____

_____

_____

_____

_____

_____

_____

_____

_____

_____

_____

_____

_____

_____

Fill in the blank.

YOU get to fill in the blank with whatever you want. YOU get to decide how your day, your week and your life is going to be. And YOU are the only one responsible for that. How it turns out is up to you. And today's version can be totally different than yesterday's, totally different than tomorrow's. YOU get to write it anyway you want.

Isn't that awesome??? And whoa, I'm not talking about defying your parents or teachers here. I'm talking about you controlling what YOU do and how YOU react to what is going on around you. Does your bedroom look like a disaster zone? Who controls that? (And remember – how you do anything is how you do everything. Messy bedroom = messy life.)

Remember the stuff about instant gratification? It's the same with getting rich or becoming wealthy or being successful in life. We want it all and we want it now. We can't wait to become a Teenager. We can't wait to graduate high school, get a job, go to College, leave home, get our own place. We're always in a rush to get 'there'.
Here's the biggest secret of all:

THERE IS NO 'THERE'

I had the pleasure of interviewing Mark Accardi, CEO of Red Brick Rentals for this book.

At his parents urging, Mark attended a Real Estate Investment seminar. He saw the money and he saw the path he wanted to take. After obtaining a Business Degree, he took various positions, all coincidently related to Real Estate investing. In his mid 20's with some help from his parents he and his brother bought their 1st investment property. Within the next year, they bought a 2nd. 7 years later their Company now owns 20 investment properties.

Coming from a middle class family upbringing Mark developed determination, drive, and focus, always with the goal of reaching the end. He soon realized that there is no end and that the journey is just as important, if not more so than 'getting there'. He was so busy concentrating on the 'end' that he didn't get a chance to fully appreciate and enjoy the journey.

I also asked Mark what the most challenging part of being a young entrepreneur is, especially when first starting out. Mark said that being taken seriously was definitely challenging, sometimes not getting Real Estate Agents to understand that he was serious. He believes it is very important to create a credible network and be mentored as well as mentor others. Collaborate with other entrepreneurs and surround yourself with other successful people.

He also believes in giving back to the community, contributing to a greater cause. Mark and his family-owned Company are doing this by building and supporting businesses that add value to the community to create a healthier lifestyle.

Every morning when you wake up, you wake up to a brand new day in your life. It is blank. YOU get to choose how that day will go. There may be outside challenges that are out of your control, but YOU get to choose how you react to them.

The Teacher throws a pop quiz at you??? No, it's not her out to get you. If you had studied the material previously, had asked for help if you didn't understand it, then you would not freak out over a pop quiz. And if you failed the pop quiz, how you handle THAT is up to you. Do you blame the Teacher? The Subject? The Test? Or do you seek out someone to help you understand it so down the road you can pass that part if it shows up on a test again?

Your future is blank. It is to be filled in by you. Through the choices you make, the habits you create and the actions you take, you get to mold your future. Your core values and how you do anything is part of the future that you get to develop and grow.

There is no one path that you must follow. But you must move. Standing still is impossible. If you start down a path and decide that's not where you want to go, take another road. You don't have to choose door number one, door number two, or door number three. Choose them all if you wish!

You most likely haven't got a clue where to start and that's okay. Just start. Think about stuff you like to do, that you are good at, that other people tell you you're good at. If you have something in mind, you have unlimited access to the resources to find out all kinds of information you might need to know about that subject, find people that have done it, people that are doing it, people that will help you do it.

Who are those people, you say?

Did you know the average of your 5 closest friends is who **you** are right now? Think about that for a bit. If everyone around you is complaining, always broke and gets into trouble at school, home or with the law, then you need to do a check on yourself.
Is that who you want to be? If it is, great! If it's not – then you seriously need new friends or someone to model yourself after.

Like attracts like. You are who you hang with.

- So who are you hanging out with?
- What are you learning from them?
- What are they learning from you?

During my interviews with many different people for research for this book, the same topic kept coming up over and over again.

MENTORS – or more importantly – the LACK of Mentors.

Joanne Carrothers of Bridge House, a community based program to help men coming out of prison get reestablished in the community, says that mentorship is a huge part of whether or not their program is successful.

I heard the same in a conversation with Donna DeJong, from the John Howard Society. The JHS runs a program called YARD – Youth at Risk Development. This program is voluntary for youth who have had a 'brush' with the law and have decided to straighten their life out. In this program, the youth establishes a rapport with a mentor and together they create and execute a plan to achieve the goals set by the youth. (Hmmm, where have I heard this before??)

It appears though that there is a huge lack of successful, business men and women and entrepreneurs that are willing to take someone under their wing, show them the ropes and hold them accountable for the goals set and the results. Or is there? Perhaps there are all kinds of business men and women willing to be mentors – they just need to be asked!

I believe part of the problem is that we don't think we can ask successful people to help us. We think they are 'too high up' to take any interest in us. But this is not what I have found in my research. The wealthy, the rich and the successful (for the most part – there are always exceptions) are very willing to share their knowledge and skills with others … and a lot of the time for free. In exchange however, they expect commitment, total engagement, and results. Their time is very valuable, so you had better be serious about accepting their generosity to help you become successful.

The other memorable comment in my research was to find a mentor that you can establish a positive working relationship with; that you, the Mentee and they, the Mentor are a good fit.

Do you have a hero? Is there someone you look up to? Do you know anyone that you want to be like?

Let's play 'What if'

- What if there were business men and women, successful entrepreneurs right in your own community that were willing to help you?
- What if your teacher, or boss where you work part time, was just waiting for you to ask?
- What if there was a famous person, a sports hero…anyone that you look up to that you could learn from virtually without actually having to meet them in person?

- What if there were Teens out there that look up to *you*, that want to be like you, and learn from you?

- What if the best mentor you could ever find lived in your home? What if it is your mom or dad, brother or sister?

  Start a conversation with your parents or older siblings who are already working. Open communication with your parents can help you understand where they are coming from, what their beliefs are about money.

Surround yourself with like-minded people, meaning people that have the same beliefs as you, that have the same ethics and similar core values, that have the traits that you want to have, whether you know them in person, or not. I have many 'virtual' mentors, that have standards, values and the integrity I want to achieve. I do what they do, I take the different beliefs, standards, skills and way of life that they have and if it is something that I want for me, I learn from them – yet I've never even met them (yet). It doesn't matter where the mentor comes from or who they are. It matters that you find one – or be one.

Not everyone will be fortunate enough to become a Teenage Money Magnet™. They won't read this book, or have the opportunity to take the program, a class or a workshop.
But you have. And you can help them. Be a mentor.
Be a hero to someone else.

You have fulfilled your promise, your commitment that you made at the beginning of this book. Congratulations! And if you didn't sign the commitment pledge at the beginning, perhaps you will do so now.

These are 10 Secrets that will make you rich or wealthy if that is what you want, and so much more - confident, self assured and successful. You are now holding the knowledge that will make sure you will never have to worry about money for the rest of your future.

Here's another little secret…

Knowledge is useless.

OMG!!!!! How could she say that???
I can hear the Teachers and Parents freaking out right now!

There's a reason I said that. Knowledge, like money is useless – unless it is **used**. Used to help make the world a better place, used to help improve the life or lives of others. If you put this book away and never do any of the things suggested in it, what good is it?
This is called "Shelf Help". It won't do you or anyone any good getting all dusty up on the shelf, just

like the million dollars won't do you any good laying under the bed.

And in the end, money is **not** everything. It is simply a tool, one of many tools that will help you become whoever you want to be.

It may open doors for you, but you have to walk through the door.

It may provide opportunities, but you have to recognize the opportunity and take advantage of it.

It may buy knowledge, but you have to know what to do with that knowledge and you have to USE IT.

In other words, it's not the money that makes you who you are, **it's you**.

The secret is knowing what to do with it.

And now you know.

And the very last thing that you need to know? Never give up. Never quit. Rearrange, regroup, take a different path, a different route…but never, ever give up on your dreams. And above all, never, ever give up on you.

The end…..

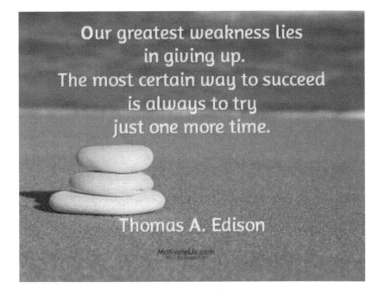

So, keep reading further! There is more valuable information in the next few pages!

RESOURCES FOR TEENS

TEEN ISSUES

- www.kidshelpphone.ca

- www.helpguide.org/home-pages/teen-issues

- www.zurinstitute.com/teenviolence

- www.bullyingcanada.ca

- kidshealth.org/teen

EATING DISORDERS

- www.bandbacktogether.com/teen-eating-disorders-resources

TEEN DRIVERS

- www.toyota.com/teendrive365

Justice for Children and Youth – Toronto

- www.jfcy.org

teens with **food allergies** and at risk for anaphylaxis.

- www.whyriskit.ca/pages/en/home.php

JUVENILE DIABETES

- www.diabetes.ca/diabetes-and-you/kids-teens-diabetes

The Gender Dysphoria Assessment and Action for Youth (GDAAY) clinic,

- www.gdaay.ca/

- www.youthline.ca

Sexual Assault in Northwest Territories

- www.justice.gov.nt.ca/VictimServices/documents/EnglishSexualAssaultBookforTeens.pdf

Please don't stop with just these few, there are SO MANY resources out there. There is help. ASK FOR IT.

Don't wait. Do it now.

EXERCISE SHEETS AND LESSONS

You can write in, or photocopy the following pages and create your own reference manual, or go to **www.theteenagemoneymagnet.com** and sign up for a membership (it's free because you bought the book!) There you can instantly download all the sheets in full size. You will also be able to download an e-copy of the book! (Just in case you lend this one to a very good friend!) Only members will have access to this. And the only way to become a member, is to read this book or take one of the workshops or programs. (Membership does have its privileges!)

Of course, the best way is to write everything down in a large notebook (a Journal), review it every 3 months and be astounded by the changes in you and your life!

If you participate in the Teenage Money Magnet™ Project, you will receive a workbook with all of this plus room to make notes.

COMMITMENT PLEDGE

I, being of sound mind and body, do hereby pledge to commit to no longer allow myself to be subject to living an ordinary life. I will not stifle my opportunities for growth and improvement, or inhibit my access to the miraculous and incredible potential lying inside me that will lead me in the direction of my greatest dreams, desires and ambitions and allow me to make a profound difference in my life, the life of my family and the world around me.

I do hereby commit to read and apply the information in this book. I will participate by reading the information, and completing all exercises.

_____

Signature

Date _____

Secret #1

What are you saying about money?

THE GOOD STUFF	THE BAD STUFF
I found $10 today!	I can't go 'cause I don't have any money.
I'm going to save up for….	I'll never be able to have …..

Change your negative money language into positive money language.

I never have any money.	I always have money.
My friends are always broke	I spend time with my friends that have money like me.
Working sucks.	I love my job

Secret # 2 – What are you Thinking?

If I could wave a magic wand and give you any amount of money you want, how much would you want?

$ _____

What would you do with that much money?

List 5 things you would do:

1. _____

2. _____

3. _____

4. _____

5. _____

You can have any amount of money you want, but you will have to earn it for yourself.

Now write down how much money you want:

$ _____

Was the second amount different from the first amount?

What would you change from your first list? What would you cross off?

1. _____

2. _____

3. _____

4. _____

5. _____

Why was the second amount different from the first?

_____

_____

_____

_____

_____

_____

_____

_____

_____

_____

_____

Write down 5 reasons why you think you can't have the amount you wrote the first time. Why was it okay if I just gave it to you, but you can't you have it if you have to earn it yourself?

I can't have $_____ because:

1. _____

2. _____

3. _____

4. _____

5. _____

List 10 people that changed the world because of thinking differently than everyone else and who made HUGE changes to the way the rest of the world now thinks and believes:

1. Einstein

2. Henry Ford

3. _____

4. _____

5. _____

6. _____

7. _____

8. _____

9. _____

10. _____

List 5 things that you once thought were true, but you don't believe anymore. (Need a couple hints: Tooth fairy/Santa/????)

1. _____

2. _____

3. _____

4. _____

5. _____

Secret # 3 – Do the Math

Take the cheque not the penny:

List the first 5 things you are going to do with that money?

1. _____

How much does it cost? _____

2. _____

How much does it cost? _____

3. _____

How much does it cost? _____

4. _____

How much does it cost? _____

5. _____

How much does it cost? _____

Secret # 5

How do people earn money?

* _____

* _____

* _____

* _____

* _____

BONUS Question:

How do YOU want to earn money?

* _____

* _____

* _____

* _____

* _____

Secret # 6

What are you afraid of? When it comes to money or anything that you don't believe you can achieve or overcome, what is it that you are REALLY afraid of?

I worry that (I'm afraid that):_____

_____

_____

_____

_____

_____

_____

_____

_____

Take your top 3 fears and write them down.

1._____

_____

2._____

_____

3._____

_____

How would you feel if you were no longer afraid?

_____

_____

_____

_____

What is the worst thing that could happen if you confronted the fear?

_____

_____

_____

_____

What is the best thing that could happen if you confronted the fear?

_____

_____

_____

_____

_____

Write down 3-5 of your Core Values

1. I must _____

2. I must _____

3. I must _____

4. I must _____

5. I must _____

Secret # 7

Make your reason profound. The Bigger the 'Why' and the more important it is to you, the better chance you will have at succeeding.

It's as simple as writing down this statement:

I want _____ because

_____

_____

_____.

Secret # 10

Today I woke up and_____

_____

_____

_____

_____

_____

_____

_____

_____

_____

_____

_____

_____

_____

_____

_____

RESOURCES
The Author Recommends

GIVING BACK (Give first, remember?)

Find a Charity or Organization that is helping to improve lives, their community, the environment, whatever you have a strong belief in, and become part of the solution. This is mine.

Teddy Bears for Tots

Teddy Bears for Tots is a Non Profit Corporation, in Hamilton Ontario.
Teddy Bears for Tots is a Non Profit Corporation, in Hamilton Ontario. Inspired to build a team of dedicated individuals bringing comfort and joy, lasting memories and smiles to children's faces by delivering Teddy Bears to McMaster Children's Hospital. Join us on our journey to make Michael's dream come true. Visit www.teddybearsfortots.com or connect with us on Facebook

CAREERS - OUTSIDE THE BOX

CONSULTING BUSINESS – Using your gifts and creating your own business. Income is earned by setting your own fees and providing various services to individuals, groups and organizations.

www.AngelWhispersConsulting.com

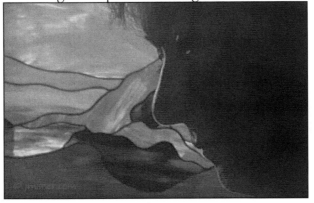

Angel Whispers was born from a dream received in 1992. This is 23 years after the start of studies and discipline of Spiritual Gifts. A Medium, Channel, Psychic, Teacher, Doreen South is an Ordain Spiritual/Christian Minister & certified Traditional Healing. She enjoyed her own live TV & radio show. Culturally inclusive. Her business offers workshops for Ontario Works, counselling through Criminal Injuries Compensation Board, and mediation for many agencies and corporations.

CAREERS OTHER THAN A JOB

NETWORK MARKETING:

Income – unlimited potential. Income is determined by how hard you work at the business.

This is one of my personal Streams of Income. You must be 18 years of age to get involved in most MLM's (Multi-Level Marketing) or Network Marketing Organizations. There are many companies out there. Do your research, pick a product you believe in, make sure the compensation plan is going to be worth the investment of your time. Above all, make sure the Company has a support system that you can depend on and provides you with all the training and help to grow your business.

Judy Willson-Simmons – Insurance Broker

Income – Unlimited Potential

An Insurance Broker is self employed and earns an income through commissions when they place or renew a policy.

Judy Willson-Simmons has been a Broker for the last 11 years. She doesn't just sell insurance policies. She helps her clients buy the RIGHT policy for their family and their needs. She is committed to her business and her clients. Her success is reflected in the number of new business, referrals and repeat clients that she establishes within her community and in Ontario.

Jennifer Rodgers – Consultant Investors Group

Young and ambitious, Jennifer has also chosen a commissioned-based career for herself.

She says she chose this profession, "To be your own boss and help people achieve their goals while sleeping soundly because their future is protected."

Investors Group

Investors Group Financial Services Inc., *I.G. Insurance Services Inc.

Jennifer Rodgers, B.A. (Hon)
Consultant

390 Brant Street, Suite 600, Burlington, ON L7R 4J4
Ph. (905) 333-3335   **Toll Free** (888) 467-8844
Fax (905) 333-3559
jennifer.rodgers2@investorsgroup.com

* License Sponsored by The Great-West Life Assurance Company

Dina Pereira – Business Owner

With her passion for doing what she loves, Dina has decided to start her own business.

Dina has been practicing and teaching yoga for over 15 years and opened Breathing Space Yoga & Wellness Services in February 2014. She is very passionate about yoga and wants to share it with everyone, to provide a space where everyone gains greater ease of body movement, flexibility, strength, awareness of breath, quieting of the mind, and nurturing of the spirit to attain inner peace and harmony. She also does Reiki, acupressure, and flower essence therapy.

Breathing Space Yoga
& Wellness Services

541 Main Street East
Main Floor
Hamilton, Ontario
L8M 1H9

289-680-9642(YOGA)
info@breathingspaceyoga.ca

ACCESS TO MORE INFORMTION

BOOKS – The Gateway to your Freedom

Whether you read them, listen to them, study them – books contain invaluable information for you to create your future IF you're reading the RIGHT books! Like these:

- The Secrets of the Millionaire Mind – T Harv Eker
- Think and Grow Rich – Napoleon Hill
- How to Win Friends and Influence People – Dale Carnegie
- The Richest Man in Babylon – George S. Clason
- Screw Business as Usual – Sir Richard Branson
- The Success Principles – Jack Canfield

Want more up-to-date stuff? These are rated the Best Sellers by Amazon

- The 7 Habits of Highly Effective Teens Workbook – Steven Covey
- The Self Esteem Workbook – Lisa M. Schab
- The Success Principles for Teens – Jack Canfield (sound familiar?)
- How to Win Friends and Influence People for Teen Girls – Dale Carnegie (hmm. Seen that title somewhere before too….)

MY VIRTUAL MENTORS

These were some of my Mentors, both virtual and actual.

I learn so much from them. Whether through seminars, workshops, books, CD's, Video – didn't matter. Check them out. Then find your own 'virtual' mentors – people that you can relate to, that you admire and have the same principles and standards you want for yourself.

- Dr. Pat Heim (she actually started me on this road!)
- Jack Canfield
- Jim Rohn
- T. Harv Eker
- Marianne Noad
- Brendon Burchard
- James Malinchak
- Barbara Stanny

ABOUT THE AUTHOR

Lynda Hykin is a self proclaimed "What-Not-To-Do" Guru, having spent most of her life broke and living paycheck to paycheck. When she found herself over 50 years old and about to become homeless, she knew that she had to make drastic changes to her life. One of those changes  was her relationship with money. Lynda now helps women and Teens learn to break the poverty cycle, create financial literacy, and discover financial empowerment.

As a Speaker, she is a recognized voice who speaks on issues of wage inequality and gender differences in the workplace, and Financial Literacy. Using her research findings and drawing on vast personal experience, she leaves audience members with enlightening and actionable ideas and insights to take control - of their money, their careers and their lives.

Made in the USA
San Bernardino, CA
10 December 2014